Missing the Rhythm King

DOLORES ANN COOPER

WestBow
PRESS®
A DIVISION OF THOMAS NELSON
& ZONDERVAN

WestBow Press books may be ordered through booksellers or by contacting:

WestBow Press
A Division of Thomas Nelson & Zondervan
1663 Liberty Drive
Bloomington, IN 47403
www.westbowpress.com
1 (866) 928-1240

Scripture taken from THE SPIRIT-FILLED LIFE BIBLE
© 2002 by Thomas Nelson Publishers.

ISBN: 978-1-9736-2892-7 (sc)
ISBN: 978-1-9736-2891-0 (hc)
ISBN: 978-1-9736-2893-4 (e)

Library of Congress Control Number: 2018905845

Print information available on the last page.

WestBow Press rev. date: 6/25/2018

To my husband, Adrian, for all his support; to my daughters,

Lisa and Cara; to my sister, Nita; and in memory of my sister,

Garcia, and my mother, Marguerite; to my brother, Eldridge; to

my grandchildren, great-grandchildren, nieces, and nephews;

and to the fans everywhere who knew and loved Eddie Gabriel.

Finally, a special thanks to my Lord and Savior, Jesus Christ

Contents

Introduction

What is known to one generation might be lost to the next. Through documentaries, books, and movies, we try to record precious memories of what we hold dear. I hold the memory of my father in my heart, and I want to express how blessed my siblings and I were to have a father like my dad. I'm compelled to pay homage to him and to give a legacy to his loved ones and adoring fans.

When I moved to Denver, Colorado, from New Orleans, people often asked me where was I from because of my accent. When I told them New Orleans, they quickly responded with exhilaration, "Oh, we love New Orleans, especially the French Quarter!"

My reply was always, "Yes, my father is an entertainer at Pat O'Brien's."

"You mean Eddie is your dad?" they would say.

The citizens of New Orleans view entertainers in the same light as doctors and pastors. Entertainment is medicine that fosters energy, and the entertainer is like a shepherd for the soul. Without music, New Orleaneans would suffer depression from the weight of the humidity and sometimes gloomy climactic conditions. While those uninterrupted rainstorms poured outside, Pat O'Brien's nightclub provided the people with Eddie the Rhythm King for great all-night entertainment.

People become famous for many reasons, and there is always something unique about what they do, which separates them and makes them stand out from others. My father was not just another accomplished musician—a great piano player, a smooth saxophone player, or a dazzling drummer. He earned his fame by creating his own unique percussion instrument that amazed and delighted people from all over the world. And for sixty-seven years, he was Pat O'Brien's special attraction. Everyone wanted to visit the French Quarter in New Orleans to see Eddie play his tray.

Chapter 1
Missing the Rhythm King

After the success of the 1955 Montgomery Bus Boycott led by Martin Luther King Jr. and the passing of the 1964 Civil Rights Act, I had two very good reasons to be jubilant. Desegregation in New Orleans had begun, and those humiliating segregation signs were removed from all over the city. I could walk into Woolworth and take my seat at the front food counter instead of walking humbly to the back of the store. Blacks hadn't even been permitted to sit down at the counters designated for them, but we were now able to sit. I couldn't wait to sit anywhere I wanted in the movie theaters—and on that most coveted front seat of the city bus. But the most important event of all was that, after twenty-seven years, I was permitted to go into my dad's workplace. I had to see for myself what tourists liked about my dad, Eddie Gabriel of Pat O'Brien's world-famous nightclub, which is located in the French Quarter of New Orleans, Louisiana.

During the late forties and mid-fifties, whenever Dad had to make a stop at work in the daytime, my siblings and I sometimes went along for the ride. But when we would arrive, we had to wait for him in the car. On his nights off, he would drive slowly down the narrow streets of the French Quarter to give us a view of the activities through the opened doors of different clubs. With neon lights flashing, virtually every *boites de nuit* (nightspot) would be ringing out live music of various kinds: jazz, calypso, rhythm and blues, Dixieland, country and western, Cajun, and popular music. New Orleans valued live music even when other cities allowed disco to put a lot of musicians out of work. The French Quarter was exciting and sizzling!

I'll never forget the day integration was put in effect, my mother enthusiastically urged us to go into Pat O'Brien's to see my dad perform. Strangely, she never cared to go, and because of our age we children weren't too bothered about the fact that we couldn't go. Segregation was just a way of life to us. However, as we got older, we became more indignant about the injustice imposed upon us "in the name of the law." Dad, however, never exhibited any kind of malice toward his employers or the segregation laws in general. He loved his job and provided everything we needed by sheer determination and a laissez-faire attitude.

My First Visit to Pat O'Brien's

In the summer of 1968, and after living seven years in Denver, Colorado, my friends and I visited New Orleans and approached the coral-red and shamrock-green building at 718 St. Peter Street. We hesitated because we saw a crowd waiting in a line a block long! Somewhat discouraged, we started to turn around and leave, but then I decided to take action. I walked up to the waiter at the door, who was busy packaging Pat O'Brien's famous hurricane glasses in souvenir boxes for the exiting fans. This prevented tourists who loved to sip and stroll in the French Quarter from littering the streets with broken glass. "I'm Eddie's daughter," I said to him. "Would you call him for me, please?"

His resounding reply was, "Eddie's daughter!" He was a young, light-skinned African American waiter in a green jacket, white shirt, black bow tie, and white pants with green stripes running down the sides. He shouted to the other waiters, "This is Eddie's daughter! Call Eddie!"

The waiting crowd looked on as we were immediately escorted into the nightclub, escaping the drudgery of standing in that endless line. That was a hallmark moment for us.

As customers left the club, new customers were hustled in, causing a constant flow of tourists in and out all night. All eyes were on us as we were led to the best table, directly in front of the stage. We felt a little apprehensive because we were the only African American folks in the newly integrated club. People were dressed up, which was customary in the clubs and restaurants of New Orleans—no T-shirts or blue jeans.

"Ed-die! Ed-die! Ed-die!" chanted the crowd. The energy was pulsating!

In walked my dad. He was smiling at the applauding crowd as he strolled with ease, holding his musical tray. He wore a shiny, sequined, Irish-green jacket with white shamrocks on the pockets. A black bow tie set off his white shirt, and green stripes ran down the sides of his white pants. However, I wondered why he was wearing sunglasses in this dimly lit nightclub, giving the impression that he was blind. Well, decades ago, he used to skillfully catch on his tray the coins that customers tossed to him. But once, one of those coins hit him in the eye. (More about that incident in a later chapter.) He also wore a toupee. Dad's hair was very fine and thin. He used to wear it slicked and combed back like Duke Ellington, but when he was between the ages of thirty-five and forty, he began losing his hair. I remember one day he was watching Mom comb my hair, and she began to brag to him how thick and long it was. He replied, "That's where all my hair went!" By that time, I knew my dad, and that comment registered as funny to me. So in order to keep a more youthful look on his job, he compensated by wearing a toupee. Therefore, the sunglasses and the toupee became part of his ensemble, giving him a "cool dude" appearance.

As I reflect on my dad's life, I am convinced that he was absolutely blessed. My mother always used to say, "You know, Daddee (as she called him) is blessed!"

The Musical Tray

Blessings in all to which you set your hand.
—Deuteronomy 28:8

In Ecclesiastes 9:10, King Solomon preaches, "Whatever your hands find to do, do it with all your might," and my dad did just that! They called him the Rhythm King, and rhythm certainly was his forte. His instrument was a large metal tray normally used to carry drinks, and he put sewing thimbles on his fingers to add his style of rhythm on his tray. This instrument was a gadget he invented for himself many years ago. The agility in his fingers was awesome. At home he would occasionally sit on a wooden chair with his hands under it and beat the rhythm to music from the radio, using his fingernails or sometimes pennies on each finger. Other times he astounded us children by showing his ability to hold fifteen soft drink bottles in each hand. Being a waiter taught him how to expedite matters by carrying the maximum number of bottles. He would place the mouths of the bottles between his fingers and thumb. Dad could tap dance, too. We were thoroughly entertained by him.

He started playing the tray in 1942 when he was only waiting tables at Pat O'Brien's. One night a customer paid his bill with loose change and put it on Dad's tray. Dad began to tap under the tray, keeping time with the piano as the coins danced. He liked the sound of it and told the piano players, "I believe I have a new act for the club! I just hope I don't mess up and drop the tray." Pennies had to take the place of his fingernails, which kept breaking. But the pennies wouldn't stay put, so he got an idea to use thimbles from watching my mother sew. He wasn't satisfied with the clanking sound made by the thimbles against the metal tray, so he creatively covered the thimbles with adhesive tape, giving it the perfect sound. Since 1942, he had worn out several dozens of thimbles, which used to cost a dime back then; today they're more than thirty cents apiece. As for his tray, he had to search extensively for the perfect combination of metals to suit him. He wore them out also with lumps and bumps from years of constant tapping.

The night he performed his first percussion act was a pivotal moment in time. Night after night, the crowd yelled for Eddie. And that was the beginning of a sixty-three-year act at Pat O'Brien's on St. Peter Street in the Vieux Carré of New Orleans, Louisiana.

Youthful and Handsome

Dad often came to our school to watch my brother run track or to pick us up when it rained since he didn't work in the daytime. My sisters and I often found ourselves convincing girlfriends that Dad was not our brother. They marveled over his youthful good looks. It made us proud to say, "No, believe me. That's my dad!"

He was always dressed in a fedora and wore neat slacks and a shirt, smelling of cologne. Neatness in appearance was very important to Dad. He reminded us that when working closely with people, one should look his or her best and smell good. However, my mother tried to explain to him that cologne should be subtle.

As he would walk out the door and leave for work, she'd yell, "You smell like the perfume factory!" Still walking, he'd yell back, "Yeah, yeah, yeah!"

That first night I went to O'Brien's, Dad climbed up on the stage sandwiched between two copper-topped grand pianos played by ladies in evening gowns. They accompanied him as he beat out the rhythm of each song. I raised my hand and waved at him. When he discovered my presence, he grinned proudly and mentioned it to the ladies on the pianos; one of them asked me to stand. "Here's Eddie's daughter from Denver, Colorado!" she shouted. The crowd cheered. That was another proud moment for my friends and me.

Smiling and moving effortlessly, Dad added his rhythm to such songs as "Yellow Rose of Texas," "Way Down Yonder in New Orleans," "When the Saints Go Marching In," "Back Home in Indiana," "California, Here I Come," New York, New York," and "Chicago," just to name a few. I was amazed at the unique sounds he made with the thimbles against the metal tray. Not only did he tap the thimbles under the tray, but he also slid them simultaneously while the coins danced. It added spice to the songs! There was a time, however, when the new owners of Pat's, presumptuously but understandably, wanted to replace my aging dad by trying to train another waiter to perform his act. Their intention was to secure the act and keep it going after Dad retired. It was a total failure! Eddie Gabriel had invented the act, he had also mastered it, and his rhythmic genre could not be duplicated. And what great rhythm he had! As for retirement, that was out of the question. He was determined to keep going, and that he did. Even to the day he died, he never missed a beat.

We sang along with everyone as we sipped the famous hurricane drink and watched my dad enjoy his job. The hurricane is Pat O'Brien's trademark drink, served in a hurricane lamp-style glass. "It is a mixture of something called Jero's Red Passion Fruit Cocktail Mix, lemon juice, and four ounces of dark rum" (Grizzard, 1978). Dad once told us the story about the time he met the famous actor Paul Newman at the club. They were in a friendly conversation while Dad was on one of his breaks. Dad asked Newman to give him the secret of his spaghetti sauce, and Newman replied, "If you give me the ingredients of the hurricane drink." They both came up empty-handed.

In 1978, when the Denver Broncos made it to the Super Bowl, Atlanta columnist Lewis Grizzard reported, "Every Bronco maniac in town for the game will have a hurricane glass before Super Bowl week is over." He added, "Two hurricanes and your average tourist is drunker than a three-eyed goat." My friends and I got a buzz just from drinking one.

I was proud of my dad. I understood why everyone wanted to see Eddie Gabriel. And that also marked the first of my countless visits to Pat O'Brien's.

Thereafter, it always pleased Dad to have his family come to Pat's to enjoy his performance and witness his talent.

Dad loved all people and they loved him. He was considered to be a "man's man," but the ladies loved him too. Dad's fame was mostly local, but it was also broadcast by tourists from around the world who came to New Orleans for Mardi Gras. His fans included such contemporaries as the famous Pete Fountain of "Licorice Stick", Al Hirt of "Struttin' Down Royal Street" and Louis (Satchmo) Armstrong of "Hello Dolly." Armstrong was Dad's idol; he had a large collection of his albums. *Louis and the Angels Sing* was a favorite. On Dad's breaks, he would walk down the street from Pat's to the famous Preservation Hall and listen to *his* favorite kind of music—Dixieland jazz, played by a pianist who everybody called Sweet Emma.

Determination
(Who Dat?)

Pat O'Brien's building was erected in 1791 and was the first Spanish theater in America (Grizzard, 1978). However, the club opened in 1933 and is equipped with a patio restaurant, a bar, and a main nightclub area with a stage. There is also an upstairs dance hall and restrooms with maids to assist patrons. It was said that many young men would give anything to wait tables at Pat O'Brien's. The founders of the club, Charlie Cartrell and Benson (Pat) O'Brien, hired my dad only after discovering that they had an extra waiter unaccounted for. Dad regaled us with the story of when he worked only as a waiter at Pat O'Brien's restaurant in 1935. Times got tough, and they had to let him and others go. He and my mother had their first baby that year, and they needed the money. Instead of giving up and going home, Dad went to the nightclub section and just started working. He didn't say a word to anyone but worked diligently for a time until one of the owners asked, "Who's that?" When Pat saw Dad's determination, he liked it and made a promise to keep him on staff as long as he wanted.

Sadly, Dad outlived both original owners and all of his coworkers. Throughout the years, he received bonuses, gifts, and big tips. On his fiftieth anniversary at Pat O'Brien's, the current owners gave him a brand new 1985 red Thunderbird. But, at seventy-eight years old, he was intimidated by the new electronics in the car, and he refused to drive it for a while. Later, he drove it only on the main streets, avoiding the fast freeways and interstates. When Dad turned eighty, I was privileged to participate in his birthday celebration at Pat O'Brien's that year. However, I made the unforgivable mistake of saying, "Daddy, you're old."

He glared at me and said in a gruff voice, "Who? I ain't old!"

I said, "But your baby girl turned fifty this year."

He looked at me and said, "Who?" It shocked him to hear that the one he had always introduced to his friends as "the baby" was now fifty years old. Anyway, *who* was his favorite word. My mother used to say to him, "The hoot owl, that's who!"

The Iron Man

Blessed shall be the fruit of your body.

—Deuteronomy 28:4

Many people called him the Iron Man. Apart from having four healthy offspring, Dad never took a day off work in sixty-seven years and was sick only once from eating contaminated lettuce from a restaurant. When asked by a newspaper columnist, after turning sixty-five, "Why haven't you retired?" his superstitious nature kicked in. He replied, "Bad things happen to people who retire. Everyone I knew who retired is now pushing up daisies" (Lind, 2001, E-1).

Next to having impeccable health, the blessing of longevity ran in Dad's family. His father died at the age of ninety-seven, his older sister died at eighty-six, his middle sister was ninety-one, and his youngest sister died when she was ninety-three.

We called Dad a health nut because he was very knowledgeable about vitamins, balanced meals, tonics, and body lotions. I gasped as I looked at his kitchen shelf crowded with bottles and bottles of vitamins: lecithin, alfalfa, selenium, and so on. Newspaper columnist Lind asked him, "How do you stay so fit?"

"Hadacol!" he laughed. "I drink Hadacol every day." (Hadacol is a popular tonic marketed by Cajun politician Dudley LeBlanc in New Orleans.) "You know why they call it Hadacol, don't you?" he asked with an impish smile. "Well, they *hadda call* it something, so they called it Hadacol" (Lind, 2001, E-1). And everyone whose name Dad could not remember was called "Hah-ya-call-em," his way of saying, "How you call him?"

Dad bathed in ammonia and sea salt, which he claimed took soreness from his muscles. I tried it once and emerged from the tub feeling very relaxed. Blackstrap molasses and vinegar were his panacea for any ailment. After Dad married my mother, he neither drank nor smoked.

O' Those Big Tips

The Lord shall command the blessings

on you in your storehouses.

—Deuteronomy 28:8

My dad reminded us that although he was on salary, it was the big tips that enabled him to send us to college and supply all our needs, above and beyond—even music and dancing lessons. There was always money in the house. Every morning, after work, Dad would bring home a large canvas sack full of his tip money: silver dollars, quarters, dimes, and nickels. He got a kick out of watching us as he dumped the large pile of coins on the bed. With wide eyes and mouths agape, we would sit and watch with visions of ice cream cones and candy bars dancing in our heads. He sat at length and counted the coins, placed them in paper rolls, and then later took them to the bank. As years went by, dollar bills replaced the coins and the tips got bigger. When my sisters and I were ready for college, we were able to pay cash for our tuition. And all three of us attended Dillard University at the same time.

Le Garçon (The Waiter)

Dining and entertainment are extremely important in New Orleans. It's a city that takes pride in good food, great entertainment, and superior service. Therefore, waiters are valuable attendants.

Traditionally, New Orleans's restaurants and nightclubs esteemed black male waiters in uniforms as emblems of Southern distinction. Dad taught us to appreciate waiters and waitresses and to tip generously. He said, "They were on their feet all day and worked hard to do their best." Not only was Dad a great musician, he was also a very good waiter. He was friendly and classy; he knew exactly how to carry himself and how to please his customers. Dentists, doctors, lawyers, and politicians who frequented Pat's would offer their services to Dad for little or no charge because he escorted them to good seats, gave them quick service, and made them feel welcomed. To this very day, my siblings and I have our own teeth because of frequent visits to Dad's dentist friends. In order to entice me back to New Orleans from Denver, Dad and Mom would boast to me that Dad knew the superintendent of New Orleans Public Schools very well. All I needed to say was, "I wanna come home," and I had a teaching job waiting for me there.

A Good Provider

But if anyone does not provide for his own, and

especially for those of his household, he has denied

the faith and is worse than an unbeliever.

—1 Timothy 5:8

Although my mother had a degree in teaching from Xavier University, she never had to use it. My dad took pride in showing her there would be no shortage of anything in our house, and he was right. We always had an abundance of everything, even bubble gum! I recall vividly that, in the forties, the corner stores were no longer selling bubble gum because of a rubber ration. Dad, who always had connections through his boss, his fans, and his friends, came home one day with a large paper bag full of bubble gum. We kids went crazy! Our jaws ached from chewing bubble gum all day. Dad was also a salesman's delight. They could have sold him the Brooklyn Bridge. One came to sell us an expensive exercise machine that vibrated as you exercised. Ironically, we were all lean, except my chubby mother, and she protested. We were the only family in the neighborhood who owned a vacuum cleaner even though we had no carpet, a motion picture camera and projector, a tape recorder, and musical instruments of many kinds (strings, bells, percussion, winds, and brass). Dad bought my brother a trumpet, hoping to say, "Blow, Gabriel! Blow!" in reference to the angel Gabriel or to follow in the footsteps of his idol, Louis Armstrong. My brother was a classmate of Ellis Marsalis Jr., father of the well-known jazz artist Wynton Marsalis. They played music together in a band at Gaudet Episcopal High School.

Music was a big part of our lives. My mother played the piano, one sister played the bell-lyre, and the other the drums, and we all tried to imitate Lionel Hampton on our xylophone. Our house was old and modest, painted coral red with French green shutters covering every window and door. It was called a shotgun house—common to the city of New Orleans. You can stand in the living room and see all the way back to the kitchen, except all the doors in each room were structured in the same position so you could not see what was going on in the rooms. So, if you stood in the front room aiming a shotgun toward the back, the bullet would meet with no obstructions. Many homes were built that way because of the lack of solid ground and for ventilation purposes. Our house had large rooms with very high ceilings. We had a large backyard with fruit trees, a side yard full of red roses and a front yard enclosed by a fence several feet from the banquette. Our street was once a canal that was later filled with transported dirt, and our sidewalks were called banquettes, pathways along a canal.

Dad's Generous Nature

Dad was free with his money. Too often, folks "put the bite on him," or took advantage of his generosity. As children, we loved shopping with Dad. At the beginning of the school year, we wouldn't get just three pairs of socks each; we'd get a dozen apiece. Mom was a little more frugal. In 1952, when Dad bought our first television set, almost every product advertised on TV found its way into our home. Many Saturday mornings, we sat in front of the TV set soaking up advertisements. Once, we heard a song about a new cereal ring throughout the house—"Kellogg's Sugar Corn Pops, sugar pops are tops!" The next morning, we giggled uncontrollably when we saw it on our breakfast table. Food was always plentiful. *Dad never came home empty-handed.* Oftentimes in the early mornings before dawn, Dad would come home from work with treats. He would wake us up by putting a "thirty-six" long oyster loaf (better known as po'boy sandwich) on French bread under our noses. Barely opening our eyes, we'd wake up grinning from the smell. It was loaded with hot, crispy-fried oysters, pickles, shredded lettuce, tomatoes, hot sauce, and mayonnaise. Other times, he would stop at the famous French market Cafe du Monde after work and bring home a large thermos full of hot *café au lait* and a large bag of hot beignets (square-shaped, fluffy, French donuts). Both

Dad and Mom cooked Italian, German, French, and the famous local dishes jambalaya and gumbo. However, we could always tell when Dad had cooked because dinner was pretty much on the spicy side, just like him.

Chapter 2

An Obedient Son

Honor thy father and thy mother, that your

days may be long and prosperous.

—Exodus 20:12

Dad was a man even at the age of ten, and everything he achieved, he had worked for. He was also very respectful, obedient, and helpful to his parents. His life was an exemplification of the above scripture. After ninth grade, Dad dropped out of school and worked to help his parents provide for the family.

He was born Eldridge Medard Gabriel on March 23, 1910, in the 1200 block of Burgundy Street, which was in the French Quarter. However, he grew up in the seventh ward of New Orleans and attended Corpus Christi Catholic Church and Xavier Preparatory High School. He was the only boy of four children born to Richard and Angelina Gabriel. He started playing the drums when he was ten years old and was once a drummer in a Dixieland band. His dad was a bass fiddler in a Dixieland jazz band, and many times Dad would help his father peddle hot rice donuts on the street corners of the French Quarter on cold winter nights. His mother was a schoolteacher and played the ukulele. She also taught in her father's private school in the French Quarter. Her father was Professor Medard Hilaire Nelson (1850–1933). He was from the West Indies with African, French, and Choctaw ancestry. He was an educator, a linguist, a humanitarian, and a philosopher who spoke seven languages. His parents spoke French in his home, and he also spoke Spanish, Italian, Portuguese, Greek, Latin, and German. He traveled extensively throughout Europe and was educated in London and Paris, and he later returned to New Orleans and opened his own school. A public school in New Orleans stands today named in his honor: Professor Medard Hilaire Nelson Elementary School. There, I was privileged to do my student teaching while attending Dillard University. However, after the Katrina flood, Medard H. Nelson was one of the many schools in New Orleans that was temporarily inoperative. It was later renovated and became one of the most modern, state-of-the-art elementary schools in the city. Dad's uncle, Francis Nelson, was also prominent as a medical doctor in Los Angeles, California, during the forties and fifties.

Creoles

You can't mention New Orleans without explaining Creoles. Both Mom and Dad were Creoles and spoke patois French, a broken mixture of French and English. We sometimes heard them speaking broken French when they wanted to keep their conversations private. Mother's favorite phrase was a combination of French and Spanish: *"Bonjour, Senor,"* which means "Good day, Lord." Until the age of six, she spoke only French and had to learn to speak English after starting school.

We grew up using French phrases and terms in our everyday conversations—*pas connaît, merci beaucoup, je ne sais pas*, and everyone was called *cher.* Even the dogs understood French. We'd yell *"Passe!"* at stray dogs, and they understood that to mean "Get away!"

It wasn't until I traveled to other cities that I realized how "French" New Orleans was, especially in my days of growing up. I recall that, in my first year of teaching in Denver, I was instructing my class on the metamorphosis of a butterfly. I pointed to a caterpillar on the board and told the class, "Take a look at the *chenille.*" A loud burst of laughter rang out from the class, and I was puzzled. "What are you laughing at?" I asked.

"You called the caterpillar a *chenille,*" laughed one boy. Unfortunately, New Orleans' French culture and traditions have faded.

There were many black high schools in the city of New Orleans, but Xavier Preparatory High was a Catholic school operated by the sisters of the Blessed Sacrament for the purpose of educating blacks and Native Americans. Louisiana, Mississippi, and Alabama were the habitation of the Choctaw Native American tribes. However, in the 1920s, most of the blacks at Xavier Prep were seventh-ward Creoles. What are Creoles? Well, the French explorer Bienville bought New Orleans and kept it from 1718 to 1769, and then he later sold it to the Spanish, who owned it from 1769 to 1803. It was then regained by Napoleon in 1800 and sold to the United States in 1803 (Martinez and Holmes, 2014). Therefore, any individual born in Louisiana with French or Spanish ancestry is considered to be a Creole. They were a clannish group who resented the Americanization of New Orleans in the early 1800s (Dufour, 1967). Even today, New Orleans has the personality of being another country, holding fast to old structures, traditions, and customs.

It was at Xavier Preparatory High School that Dad met my mother, Marguerite Blanche Clizac. She was the only child of John and Cornelia Clizac. She too was a musician and played the piano. She was of Indian, French, and African ancestry. My dad boasted, "She was crazy about me because I was a drummer for our school's band." And he was right! My mother was in love with my dad. Her favorite song for him was, "I'll Get by as Long as I Have You." They were married in 1932. She was a good wife and an excellent stay-at-home mom. Dad was a man of integrity and found a way to keep every promise he made. Before the death of my mother's parents, my dad made a promise to my dying grandmother that he would always take care of my mother. And for forty-seven years, until she passed away in 1979 of amyotrophic lateral sclerosis (ALS), better known as Lou Gehrig's disease (named for the beloved New York Yankee baseball player), he did just that.

Dad and Mama enjoyed a life influenced much by the French culture, especially the popular phrase *Laissez les bon temps rolle*, which means, "Let the good times roll!" They attended debutante and carnival balls, horseracing, Creole festivals, holiday dinners, and football games, but most of all, they enjoyed their four children.

A Protective Dad

The rod and rebuke give wisdom.
—Proverbs 29:15

Life with my dad was interesting and fulfilling. Jokingly, we called him Dracula because he worked nights from 7:00 p.m. to 4:00 a.m. and slept during the day. We had to be quiet most days, but when sibling rivalry occurred, he didn't "spare the rod." There were times when all he had to do was reach for his trousers next to his bed, rattle his belt, and stomp one foot hard on the floor. That sound alone would silence us. He was a good dad—a gentle, easygoing fellow—and it gave him no pleasure to whip us. One day, he came home with a brand new 1952 Plymouth. My oldest sister, who had not even so much as a learner's permit and was only fifteen years old, begged him to let her drive it. Without hesitation, he agreed. I jumped in and went on the joyride. Excited and full of adventure, she drove down London Avenue near one of New Orleans's notorious pumping stations of the London canal. The street is now known as A.P. Tureau Street. Suddenly, she hit a big pothole. The car veered out of control and hit a parked car, causing damage to the right front of my dad's new car. We got out, left the car there, and walked home. My sister was worried and cried all the way. When my dad heard what had happened, he didn't say a word; he just walked down the street to retrieve the damaged car. My sister and I were so relieved. I remember how it warmed my heart when he didn't chastise her. I admired him for it. I learned a little more about who my dad was. I had never seen him anxious or baffled about anything. He always maintained a cool head.

Sometimes I used to beg him to let me drive his new blue and white 1956 Buick to school, just to exercise my independence and show off to my classmates. Once when he let me, I was driving down an overpass going much too fast and was unable to come to a complete stop, and I ran into the back of a Renault Dauphine that was waiting at a red light. The Buick's strong metal bumper totaled the Renault's engine, which was in the back. The policeman was ready to take my new license, but then my dad slyly pulled him aside and whispered something to him. The next day the newspaper reported that I had suffered a minor injury and had been released from the hospital. Not true! I suffered no blame, was more like it. My dad had greased the cop's hand. His favorite words of wisdom were "Money talks." The only correction I got was, "Next time, pump the brakes!"

However, another example of his doting was when I had my first child by cesarean section; there was a very impatient, angry nurse who had no sympathy for the aftermath of such an operation. I mentioned it to my dad, and he asked me to point her out. Later, he pulled a few strings, and the next day she came into the room with such a great transformation of attitude; she was syrupy sweet and overly helpful. I couldn't bear it!

Like a big brother, he handled our conflicts many times. And was extremely protective of us. One incident was particularly menacing for the entire family. One of my sisters was a victim of a phone stalker who called her repeatedly every day for several weeks. He would remain silent, listening for her voice, and then breathe heavily before viciously hanging up on her. Those menacing calls went on for weeks. It became so annoying that we were afraid to answer our phone. It was all we could think about. We reported it to the Southern Bell telephone company many times. Fortunately, one operator was very cooperative and determined to go the extra mile for us. The operator stayed on our line until she caught him. She was able to trace the call and give us the phone number and address of the culprit. Dad did not call the police, yet he wasted no time getting up from his daytime sleep. He calmly dressed, went out to his car, and drove to the house of this menacing suspect. We girls waited inside the car and watched Dad boldly walk up the front steps of the suspect's house. He confronted him at his front door face to face. We didn't hear what he said, but from the sheepish look on the young man's face, it spoke volumes. From that day on, we had no more phone calls from that individual.

Dad faithfully attended all of our dance recitals, which were presented by the Seventh Ward's prominent Audrey Mae Dumas Dancing School. Dad spent a lot of money on our dancing lessons, tap shoes, and costumes. He also never missed my brother's track meets. And in 1953, when my brother joined the US Marine Corps, Dad and Mom wore "I like Ike" buttons in support of Dwight D. Eisenhower simply because Eisenhower campaigned to bring an end to the Korean War.

My dad was very supportive of all of our endeavors and very protective of us as well. As a child, I loved to sit at our dining room table and draw pictures. Later, Dad provided money for me to enroll in a commercial art correspondence course and took me to the famous Jackson Square on Decatur Street so that I could sketch the St. Louis Cathedral. He painstakingly sat with me the entire time, making sure no harm came to me. A few artists who often congregated in the square stopped by to view and critique my drawing. One suggested to Dad, "Give her to me. I'd be happy to help her develop her drawing skills." Dad replied, "Naw!" and abruptly turned away from the man. When we got home, I overheard him relate the incident to my mother: "'Give her to me,' he said. What kind of fool did he think I was!" he griped. Because of Dad's encouraging efforts to support my art, I won a tuberculosis poster contest at my high school. It was a city-wide competition that was reported on in the New Orleans *Item-Tribune* newspaper. Mom showed Dad the article with my name as a recipient of a merit award, and Dad cleared his throat as he read it. He had a habit of clearing his throat when he was proud of something.

A Better Home

Dad decided it was time to stop renting and buy his family our own home. To keep us busy and out of the streets during the summer months, he opened up a sweet shop in the front of the house for us to work in. We didn't like working in it, but we enjoyed dancing to the jukebox and eating the sweets. "Y'all eatin up all ma profit!" he complained. My sister and I looked at each other and asked, "What's that?" That was the first time I learned what *profit* meant. Eventually, our shop became notoriously popular with teenagers and some riffraff from all over the city, so Dad took out the jukebox and turned the shop over to our grandfather Poppa, who was also my godfather and whom I also adored. After the shop did not prove profitable, for tax purposes as well as extra income, Dad built a laundromat next door to it. However, Mom always advised him that in order to have a successful business, he had to be there to initiate it. "You can't be two places at once," she'd say. The laundromat survived for a little while, but the customers became bothersome. They would knock on our door at all hours of the day and evening asking for change or complaining about the machines.

Morals and Values

Although Dad was a man of few words and very candid in his approach, when he gave advice, it was solid and no one could argue with it. Once, my sister was battling with two suitors. While my mother labored over which one should be the one, my dad spouted out, "Leave them both alone!" Fortunately, Dad and Mom imparted Judeo-Christians values to us coupled with everyday wisdom. However, Dad particularly stressed independence. "Be independent," he'd say. "That way you won't be beholden to nobody." He claimed education would give us a handle on independence. At that period in time, the city of New Orleans had approximately eleven colleges and universities, three of which were primarily black. My oldest sister graduated with a BS degree in nursing, and I graduated with a BA degree in education from Dillard University. My other sister finished her education in New York with a BA degree. My brother felt that his training in the US Marine Corps was his stepping stone to a better life, and he later traveled all over the world, to France, Austria, Switzerland, Japan, Italy, Israel, and so on.

I recall when my two sisters decided to get jobs while they were in college. They applied at a store on Canal Street where our main shopping center was located. They were hired to be elevator girls at a lady's store called Goldrings. Elevator attendants were popular in the fifties; the doors had to be opened manually. I was envious of their newfound freedom and independence. Every time I saw them in their uniforms of black nylon dresses with gold rings on the pockets, I sulked. Their salaries were small but gave them an air of self-worth. I said to my dad, "I want a job." He barked, "No! You don't need to work at your age. You better concentrate on finishing school because when you are an adult you'll be working for the rest of your life!" Ooh, that had such a "life sentence" ring to it. After hearing that, I never pestered him again about getting a job. As a matter of fact, I didn't obtain a social security card until I graduated from college.

It was a French custom to drink wine with meals, even though we did so only for holidays. Yet, Dad cautioned us girls, "Don't ever get drunk!" He believed a lady could never exonerate her reputation if she did. "A man could get drunk," he would say, "fall in the gutter for all to see, and the next day he would still be respected as a man. Not so with a woman." We heard that song many times. And he always cautioned, "Whatever you do, don't mess with people of God!" ("Do not touch my anointed and do my prophets no harm" (1 Chronicles 16:22).)

Chapter 3
Segregation

Before integration and the civil rights movement, Pontchartrain Beach, the city's amusement park, was for whites only. It grieved me as a child every time my dad drove pass Pontchartrain Beach on our way to the African American section of the lake. It was the one thing about the segregation laws I hated the most— watching the bright lights of the roller coaster full of children screaming with joy from the thrill of the ride.

At the movie theaters, there were segregated sections. We had to sit in the balcony, and the Lowe's State Theater on Canal Street had an extremely steep balcony. We kids called it the "falling down theater." The head of the person in front was at the feet of the person sitting behind. We were afraid to walk up or down for fear of falling all the way over the balcony onto the folks below. Dad would securely hold our hands and sit us on his lap. Nevertheless, thanks to my dad, we didn't grow up hating or holding malice in our hearts for anyone because of race, color, or creed. We learned to handle people as individuals, and Dad saw to it that we had all that we needed. That's not to say that Dad wasn't exposed to bigotry or hatred. Indeed, he was. The incident involving the coin that hit him in the eye while he was performing on his job was a deliberate act of racism. That drunken individual also spouted a racial slur and was booted from the club immediately. This was a rare occurrence at Pat O'Brien's. I believe my dad maintained his positive attitude simply because of decent people like Pat O'Brien and Charlie Cantrell, who didn't tolerate racism against their employees. Incidentally, Dad tried not to put himself in a position to gripe or complain about the lack of anything. He never even rode the segregated city buses because he always had a good, running car.

Dad made our fun. And we were never idle! He took us to the circus and to the annual fair every summer. These brought out the child in him. At the fair, he rode all the rides with us. On the Rock O' Plane, every time we flipped upside down, his sundry coins spilled out of his pocket onto the ground. We all laughed as the young boys below went crazy scurrying to pick them up.

Mardi Gras

Because the carnal mind is enmity against God; for it

is not subject to the law of God, nor indeed can be.

(Romans 8:7)

The term *mardi gras* is French for "fat Tuesday." This French Catholic celebration epitomizes New Orleans: *Dum vivimus, vivimus!* ("While we live, let us live it up!") It is by no means a spiritual event, but it is certainly "religious and ritualistic." The word *carnival* comes from the Latin word *carnalis* meaning "flesh" and representing the carnal-minded man, rather than the spiritual man. The flesh man carouses during the entire carnival season with parades, balls, drinking, eating, and so on. And Mardi Gras is the culmination of all of the carousing. Ash Wednesday, which follows, is the beginning of the forty-day Lenten period. This was promulgated by the Catholic Church, which commissions the parishioners to fast and pray during this forty-day period before Easter Sunday. During Lent, we didn't dance or listen to our rock and roll or rhythm and blues music.

Mardi Gras was always a fun time for us. During the carnival season, Dad made a lot of money. I remember one year when Dad masqueraded at Pat O'Brien's as the famous pirate Jean Laffite.

Tourists from all over the world came to the Mardi Gras.

Dad would find time to take us to the exciting night parades, putting us on his shoulders to catch beads and trinkets thrown by the men in masks riding the beautifully decorated floats. Early in the morning at the crack of dawn on Mardi Gras, we would peek out our window to see the parade of colorfully decorated Indians in their elaborate costumes, which took all year to make. These men were African Americans who claimed to have Native American ancestry. They traveled in packs; each pack belonged to a different tribe, and they competed fiercely with one another over who had the prettiest costume. It sometimes got unruly, so we children kept our distance.

Dad worked day and night on Mardi Gras. However, he would park his car on the neutral grounds of Claiborne Street, which was where mostly Seventh Ward people liked to gather. There our family sat in the car, rested, and picnicked. It was long before the city constructed Interstate 10 over the spacious neutral grounds that were full of palm trees. We also walked all the way to Canal Street, which was the route of Rex, the Mardi Gras king. We walked through a large portion of the city in our masquerade, and at the end of the day, we would have the traditional Mardi Gras meal: red beans and rice with smoked sausage.

The next day, however, Catholics from all over the city were recognizable by the ashes on their foreheads. This was to solemnize that we came from ashes and to ashes we shall return.

Superstitions

Dad was a decent man. He was trustworthy, God fearing, and law abiding for the most part, except when it came to "greasing the hands" of policemen. However, he never went to jail in all of his ninety-five years. As a child, Dad learned the law of reciprocity. Aside from believing that money talks, he always gave money to anyone in need. ("Give and it will be given to you good measure, pressed down, shaken together, and running over will be put into your bosom for with the same measure that you use, it will be measured back to you" (Luke 6:38).) He gave money for my mother to adopt children from the Maryknoll Fathers of the Catholic Charities via mail order and to family members and friends in need. My mother often claimed, "The reason Daddee is so blessed is because he has an opened hand, free to give and receive." However, Dad had his share of shortcomings and peculiarities.

No one's perfect, and Christians are no exception. We're just redeemed through faith in Jesus Christ, not by our goodness, lest anyone should boast (Ephesians 2:9). As long as we are in this tabernacle of clay, we are susceptible to errors. New Orleans is predominantly Catholic, as the first settlers of Louisiana were from Catholic-dominated countries such as France, Spain, Italy, Ireland, and Yugoslavia.

Catholicism was the stepping stone of my faith in Jesus, but common among many Catholics is their superstitious beliefs, which sometimes rule their decisions. Dad hung rosary beads in his car for protection, and he knelt before statues, lit big vigil candles at their feet, and attended novenas. After the death of my mother, he was so grieved and missed her so much that he continued to burn twenty-four-hour vigil candles for her soul. At night, this was the only shining light in the house. He believed in praying for the souls in purgatory, a Catholic doctrine. He also wore a St. Christopher's medal around his neck, representative of the saint popularly known in New Orleans as the saint for travelers. He carried a rabbit's foot and cloves of garlic in his pocket, and he also ate a lot of garlic, which I'm sure kept a lot of demons away! He bought "holy water" from the priest's rectory to bless our house, and over every door was either a horseshoe or a cross made from palms of the previous year's Palm Sunday. Mother too had statues of Mary and pictures of Jesus painted by Italian artists all over the house.

Dad was a paradox. He was a faithful Christian, yet he toyed with astrology, followed his daily horoscope, and made many decisions based on its predictions. He sometimes startled us children with his superstitious convictions. I recall vividly one day playing jacks with a friend, and Dad woke from his daytime sleep. On his way to the bathroom, he caught me as I rested both hands on my head while I sat on the floor. He yelled at me, "Take your hands off your head! You want your mama to die?" I immediately dropped my hands and glared at him, feeling a tinge of guilt. We were never allowed to put scissors or hats on the bed. We didn't dare open an umbrella in the house, we never kneeled unless to pray, and we couldn't have a bird in the house, caged or loose. Our house had three exits—front, side, and back. On occasion, we would leave the side door, which had no screen, open. Once in a while, a sparrow would fly into our house, and Dad would make the sign of the cross and shout, "Get that bird outta here! A bird in the house, poor as a louse."

He was also convinced that people who practiced witchcraft could put hexes on others through some act of sorcery called "the evil eye." However, contrary to popular beliefs, he considered our beloved black cat, Lacy, to be a lucky charm.

In his younger days, he and my grandfather, as well as many parishioners in the Seventh Ward of Corpus Christi church, used to visit Marie Laveaux's grave on All Soul's Day, the day after Halloween. She was a well-known French-mulatto voodoo priestess with a spirit of divination who practiced necromancy. She was also a devout Catholic and had a large entourage in the city of New Orleans.

The Accident

Dad sometimes acted hastily and wasn't one to shy away from risks. My mother tried to be a guiding influence in his life. Sometimes she succeeded, and other times she failed. One summer, our family was preparing to join a group of relatives and friends for a Fourth of July picnic at the Abita Springs resort in Slidell, Louisiana, a place Dad often took us swimming. It had a huge circular swimming pool surrounded by spacious grounds with lots of trees and picnic tables. Everyone was scheduled to ride a chartered bus, except Dad. He preferred taking his car and trying to arrive before the bus. He took a shortcut on a dirt road and occasionally hit a few bumps. Mother cautioned him many times about speeding on a dirt road. She was in the front seat with Dad, and my two sisters and I were in the back seat. Fortunately, my brother was away at Boy Scout camp. I was ten years old and had learned to swim that year in Lake Pontchartrain, so I was eagerly looking forward to swimming in the big round pool again. I leaned my head against the back window on the right side, lulled to sleep by the forward motion. While I slept, I could feel the sensation of bouncing up and down, thinking it was the bumps in the road. Suddenly, I felt pain in my head and heard my mother screaming for me, "My baby! My baby!" When I realized that the car was upside down, I panicked and cried out for my mother.

Dad had raced across some railroad tracks, causing the car to flip over three times! It landed on its top. Dad and Mother got out first and began to pull us out of the upside-down, dark, dusty, and hot car. No one was seriously injured—just cuts, bumps, and bruises. It was not luck but a true blessing, considering there were no seat belts in those days. Mother ran out into the wide open field, fell on her knees with her arms lifted up, and shouted, "Thank you, Jesus!" Tears streamed down her face. My sisters and I followed close beside her. Dad was ashamed and sat silently in the gutter, looking at his upside-down car and shaking his head. A passerby picked us up and took us to the resort, but we weren't allowed to swim because of our injuries and for fear of polio and lockjaw, which were threatening in those days.

Chapter 4
A Premonition

Pat O'Brien's most prosperous and busiest times of the year were the Mardi Gras season, Super Bowl Sunday, St. Patrick's Day, Bayou Classics, the New Orleans Jazz Festival, Christmas Eve, and New Year's Eve.

In years past, I have spent several Christmases in New Orleans with my mom and dad, but in December 2004, I was compelled to spend Christmas exclusively with my dad. I told my husband, "I need to visit my dad. At his age, he could go any day now, even in his sleep. He doesn't have to be sick." I felt a strong urge to see him. I even quit my job teaching at a tech college. If I didn't return to work, that would have been automatic dismissal. I didn't care; it was more important to me to check on my dad.

As a child, Dad and Mama made Christmas and all holidays a

joy for our family. It is the celebration of the birth of Jesus Christ, and for these very reasons I love Christmas!

My husband, of whom my dad approved very much, and I traveled from Denver to New Orleans in our bus, which we had converted into a motor home. When we arrived, New Orleans was experiencing one of its rare snow flurries. The previous one was the 1965 snowfall. Dad didn't want us to stay in the bus. They owned a modest three-bedroom brick home, *crowded* with expensive and elaborate possessions, but he insisted that we stay in one of their bedrooms. He had become cantankerous in his old age, and it didn't pay to argue with him. I'm glad I didn't. It gave us a chance to spend quality time with him. Other times, we would just pop in at Pat O'Brien's to see him. Anyhow, it turned out to be one of our most enjoyable Christmases. Not only did he have his daughter there, but his great-granddaughter and his great-great granddaughter were also there spending his last Christmas with him. Dad regaled us with amusing tales, some of which I had heard many times before, but one story in particular was, in retrospect, an eerie presage, to say the least. He told us of how his paternal grandmother, who was a Native American, had drowned in the Mississippi River. She was known in the village for visiting everyone before going home, and many times she washed her clothes in the river. One day she didn't return home, and her husband and others thought she was still out visiting so they didn't go out to search for her. They later found her body floating in the river. It was determined that she had drowned.

Dad was ninety-four years old, and it amused me to see him eating anything he wanted: cookies, Snickers, ice cream and cake, and even spicy gumbo. They didn't call him Iron Man in vain; he had an iron stomach!

Dad loved animals, mostly cats. So I was surprised to meet his three dogs. Two were vicious little Chihuahuas. They growled at and bit anyone who came near him. I learned that the hard way! One day, Dad was lying in his huge, four-poster bed with satin sheets looking like a king. I went up to him, moving abruptly, and one of his little dogs dashed from under the bed and bit my ankle.

He named the two little Chihuahuas Me and You. The other dog was a mild-mannered fat dachshund he had named Two in One.

One night my husband got up to use the bathroom. The little dog named You was growling while guarding the bathroom door, which was closed. Not knowing my dad was in the bathroom, and not wanting to provoke the dog to bark, my husband got back in bed, sighing.

I asked him what was the matter.

He replied, "I need to use the bathroom."

I said, "Go ahead!"

He answered, "You won't let me."

I asked, "Who, me?"

He said, "No, You."

For months we had fun with those two names.

My dad was fortunate in his choice of wives. My stepmother was also a dependable wife. She helped Dad dress, combed his toupee, cooked healthy meals, and drove him to and from work. I remember suggesting to my dad that he not remarry after my mother died.

I said, "Dad, why don't you remain single and just travel the world?"

He said, "No, I need someone to take care of me in my old age." I couldn't argue with that.

Each night my stepmother and I stayed up until four o'clock in the morning, talking and waiting for the time to pick Dad up from Pat O'Brien's. He rarely drove his car. His gait was weak and unsteady, and he was thin and shrunken. As I watched him dress for work—still natty, though—I had flashbacks of him when he was young and strong, smelling of cologne. I waited until You was out of biting distance, and I reached for my dad (not knowing it would be the last time) and hugged and kissed him on his sunken cheek. He laughed, but my heart ached to feel his fragile shoulders. He even had to wear suspenders to keep his pants up. However, when we dropped him off in front of the nightclub, he deliberately straightened his back, lifted his steps high, and strutted up the curb to the entrance. My stepmother and I looked at each other and laughed. "So! It's Pat O'Brien's that's keeping him going!" I squawked. I recall a conversation that Dad had with my brother-in-law. He yelled at Dad, "Man! Can't you talk about anything else besides Pat O'Brien's?" Dad just laughed. This is the main reason Dad could not maintain a business; he couldn't give up Pat O'Brien's.

For the most part Dad spent his days at home in bed watching television with his favorite dog, You, by his side, and his nights were spent at Pat's. However, he seemed melancholy and didn't talk as much as he once did. I couldn't decipher whether it was due to the death of my sister, who died of breast cancer in 2002, or just that he was tired of living. I couldn't discuss it with him; I didn't want to sadden him with more, since grief can kill a man at his age. He never expected in his whole life that he would have to bury any of his beloved children.

New Year's Eve

New Year's Eve was drawing near, and Pat O'Brien's anticipated a large crowd. My stepmother was worried about how Dad was going to get to work through the barricaded streets of the French Quarter. He would have to walk a few blocks. Impossible! I worried, and I refused to be satisfied until they allowed him to be driven up to Pat's front entrance. I suggested, "Explain to the guards who he is, and then insist!" Crime had increased drastically in New Orleans. And although Dad carried a gun, he never used it, but the thought of my little ol' weak dad walking alone several blocks from Pat's was frightening. He once told us a story about the time he was in a rough section of town pumping gas in his car when a suspicious character walked toward him with a cigarette in one hand and the other hand in his pocket. The man came from out of nowhere and asked Dad, "Do you have a light?" Before the man could get closer, my dad pulled out his gun and said, "Put the cigarette in your mouth, and I'll light it from here." The man took off running.

Last Goodbye

The holidays were coming to a close, and my husband and I decided to spend New Year's Eve with friends in Texas. It was a dreary, overcast day. We all hugged, kissed, and walked toward the bus. I turned around and looked back at my dad and stepmother as they stood together waving goodbye from their front yard in the heart of the lower Ninth Ward. Even after I got on the bus, I moved to the back window but couldn't stop looking back. I didn't know it was the last time I would see my dad, but in the back of my mind I sensed that it could be. However, I didn't in my wildest thoughts believe that a terrible flood would take his life. I wanted to go back and give him one more hug, but I didn't want to alarm him. I feel blessed to have spent his last Christmas with him. Thinking back, many times Dad would drive me to the airport, sending me off after my Christmas visits, and put money in my hand just before boarding the plane.

They stood side by side watching us until we drove out of sight. Feeling sad, I fought back tears and tried to concentrate on finding our way to Interstate-10 from that fateful lower Ninth Ward.

The Ninth Ward

I hadn't spent much time in the Ninth Ward and was not familiar with the area. Our family had grown up in the Seventh Ward. Three years after my mother died in 1979, Dad remarried and moved to the lower Ninth Ward. One of my favorite rock and roll singers, Fats Domino, who is famous for his song "Blueberry Hill," also lived in the Ninth Ward. When we moved to our own house on North Galvez Street, which was the main thoroughfare to the Ninth Ward, we used to sit on our porch and watch for Fats Domino to speed by in his pink Cadillac, with his name painted across the doors. "Hey, Fats!" we'd all yell out to him. He would reply by giving us a long honk on his horn.

After every New Orleans's hurricane, the Ninth Ward was always flooded with at least three to four feet of water. The Industrial Canal pumping station was only a few blocks away from Dad's house, and it was a major cause of floods when it overflowed. Many people who lived in that section of town had flood insurance and were forever remodeling their floors after a flood.

While in Texas, I called my stepmother to inquire about Dad and how he had been able to get to work on New Year's Eve. It was a blessing! A policeman on horseback had removed the barricades to allow her to drive Dad up to the entrance of Pat O'Brien's on St. Peter's Street.

A Good Swimmer

Growing up in a city surrounded by water, my dad had learned to be a good swimmer and taught us to swim. He took us swimming to various places: Abita Springs in Slidell; Waveland, Gulfport, and Biloxi, Mississippi; and many times to Lake Pontchartrain, which spilled over into the Gulf of Mexico. Dad would sit high on the top steps of the levy and take videos of us swimming and diving into the lake, which seemed like an ocean to us. As children we didn't realize we were living in the swamps, so to speak, "five feet under the sea." I remember how exciting, but frightening, my first airplane flight over New Orleans was. I couldn't believe my eyes as I looked down at the huge bodies of water surrounding New Orleans while the plane was descending, which explains why most of New Orleans's gravesites are crypts and tombs above the ground. There were many tales told about caskets that had been buried six feet underground later found floating in the Mississippi River after heavy rains. Thus came the practice of burying above ground. Fortunately, my mother and sister are buried in the new mausoleums. From January 2005 to August 2005, I spoke to my dad four times by phone: once in January, then for his birthday in March, another for Father's Day, and once in the two weeks before that terrible Katrina flood of August 29. He had become hard of hearing, so our telephone conversations were brief.

Hurricane Katrina

On Monday, August 29, 2005, my ninety-five-year-old dad was still an employee of Pat O'Brien's when he succumbed to Hurricane Katrina. He rarely took a day off and was still healthy and alert.

The weekend before the levy broke, August 27, 2005, my daughter, who was my dad's beloved first grandchild, saw on the news that there was a threat of a category five storm approaching New Orleans. She spoke several times to her grandfather and his wife, urging them to evacuate or get on higher ground. Before Hurricane Betsy had hit New Orleans in 1965, my dad had taken my mother uptown to a hotel near Canal Street. My daughter thought he might consider doing the same thing while Katrina was ominously approaching. His reply was, "I've been through a lot of hurricanes—Hurricane Betsy and Hurricane Camille, and the storm of 1915. I helped my younger sister to safety. Anyway, only God knows what will happen." Those were his last words to her. Upon hearing that, my daughter became frantic and called me several times to express her concern. Regretfully, I felt no urgency to convince them to leave. Oftentimes, God spared New Orleans from hurricanes. It always blew over the city, and the most damage done was a few broken tree limbs and a few feet of water around town. So, if people around the world wondered why so many refused to leave the city, it was because there had never been a threat of the levy breaking since Hurricane Betsy, and even at that time it held up. It was said that Hurricane Betsy cost the city one billion dollars in damage (Dufour, 1967).

I called my dad to try and persuade him to go to a hotel, but in no time at all the circuits became busy. At a point when I could not reach them, I assumed Dad had taken precaution and gone to higher ground. The urgency of the storm was not expressed as much in Denver's media as it was in New Orleans.

There was no entertaining at Pat O'Brien's that night. The city literally shut down due to the anticipation of a category five hurricane. It was reported that approximately 490,000 people had evacuated the city and about 10,000 remained. The highways were crowded with desperate motorists trying to leave the city. Many who stayed didn't want to fight that catastrophe, yet unfortunately met with one that was more grievous.

Even with all the media warnings, my stepmother, who had had several heart bypasses, and my dad, who was ninety-five years old, told everyone they decided to remain in their lower Ninth Ward home and ride out the storm.

For nine days, my family and I didn't know if my dad and stepmother had survived the flood. Circuits for both land phones and cell phones were either busy or down. It was the most frustrating and heartrending time of my life.

I consulted my computer day and night, searching at length for word of my dad and his wife. I even posted a message appealing to anyone who may know of his or her whereabouts. I felt totally helpless. I sent emails to Pat O'Brien's, KatrinaVictims.com, and NOLA.com, but to no avail.

Ironically, Dad had once told us that people often said to him when they hadn't seen him in a long time, "Man, I thought you were dead!" His reply was, "I ain't gonna die, I'm gonna do like the male donkey and disappear." People laughed when they heard this, but it took me a long time before I understood this adage. For the sake of clarity, donkeys cannot reproduce themselves; consequently, that species just disappeared. This statement, however, foreshadowed the events that followed the flood. I was holding onto rumors in hopes that my dad was still alive. On September 2, 2005, information from the computer stated that he was rescued and taken to Slidell, but I heard rumors that he was seen on TV fighting rescuers, not wanting to leave New Orleans.

After several anxiety-riddled days, on September 6, 2005, I got a call from my sister in New York giving me the phone number of a nursing home in Arkansas where my stepmother had been taken. Finally, I made contact with her, but my countenance fell and I went from joyful to sorrowful in a second when she told me my dad had drowned; they could not find his body. She was totally irrational and out of sorts. It took several conversations with her before she sufficiently regained her memory to relate a little more of what happened that horrible night.

That Horrible Night

According to my stepmother, Dad was prepared for at least a few feet of flooding because, for safety's sake, he had the attic ladder pulled down. That evening they both prayed at the foot of the ladder before going into the kitchen for dinner. They sat in the light of a kerosene lamp and listened to the forceful wind and rain beating heavily on the roof and windows. It was the worst storm they had ever heard. Then the hurricane gradually came to a halt. They were relieved; the storm was over. But then, suddenly, they heard a loud boom! Water rushed into the house from everywhere, breaking out doors and windows. And before they could react, the water was almost to the ceiling. Shocked and panicky, they struggled to move from room to room, but since there were no lights, they couldn't tell which direction they were headed. The dark waters were forceful, and everything was floating. They tried to maneuver to the front door, but something was blocking it. At some point, Dad got caught between their two refrigerators yet somehow broke loose. He desperately held onto his wife's hand; she could not swim.

As my stepmother related her account of the tragedy to me, I had flashbacks of a time when I was twelve years old and had tried to save another child from drowning in deep water. I jumped into the swimming pool to rescue her, but she panicked and began to climb on top of my head, pushing me under over and over until a lifeguard had to rescue both of us.

While holding her hand, Dad was trying to make his way to the attic ladder that he had previously pulled down in the hallway near their bedroom. The weight of the floodwaters was too heavy and forceful for a ninety-five-year-old man struggling to swim with his wife. After pushing her to the ladder, weak and out of breath, his grip loosened on her hand. He began to choke on the water and started sinking, and the strong current swept him away. Left hanging on the ladder, my stepmother was horrified! Yet she climbed to safety and lived to give an account of that horrible night. She spent a long, dark night in the attic of their home in a state of shock, listening to things below bumping around in the moving waters.

Still in a state of shock, she could not recall precisely what happened. The next day, rescuers came in boats, and she told them that Dad was still in the house. She didn't know if they had gone down into the flooded house to try to find him, but she did believe that he had drowned. "He's gone," she said to me.

The Superdome

My stepmother was taken to the Superdome before she was transported to Arkansas. That was another horrific experience for her. For five days, she was traumatized. "It was miserable!" she gasped. Decent people had to mingle with low-life criminals. There was no food or water for five days, and being a diabetic, this put her life in jeopardy. She claimed it was by the grace of God she survived. The air was foul and contaminated. The ninety-eight-degree heat was unbearable, and many of the elderly succumbed because of it. Babies cried, and women and children were ravished. Many people died, and their bodies were left uncovered. All she heard was groaning, weeping, and promises of help.

People around the world expressed indignation at the hungry people of New Orleans breaking into stores to steal food. I call those people "nicer than God." For even God said, "People, do not despise a thief if he steals to satisfy himself when he is starving" (Prov. 6:30). On the other hand, I was appalled, but not surprised, at the deranged characters wading through chest-deep waters carrying stolen TV sets. What a farce!

Evacuees

Some evacuees from New Orleans were transported to Denver's old Lowry Air Force Base. Barefoot, dirty, and penniless, these people were devastated, uprooted to an unfamiliar city with no belongings but just the clothes on their backs that they had worn for an entire week. They had left a city that was 80 percent flooded with homes still six to eight feet under water. Many loved ones drowned in attics and in the city streets. And at this writing, many claim some family members are still missing. In spite of all this, I consider the survivors blessed because their lives were spared, giving them another chance to make a new start.

Overwhelmed with my own grief, I was eager to help them in any way I could. I went to the base seeking to put my arms around them and tell them how sorry I was. To my disappointment, they were heavily guarded, and no one was allowed in the barracks except the Red Cross crew or people from other charitable organizations. I gave Red Cross my phone number and offered my availability to the evacuees for shelter, clothing, and food.

Our Claims for Compensation Denied

Two years later, the federal government, with the intentions of helping the dispersed citizens of New Orleans come back home, initiated a program called the Road Home. This program offers what is called a forgivable loan to the flood victims whose homes were destroyed. It requires the recipient to get a loan from any participating bank offering the best interest rates, and they must do everything dictated by the Federal Emergency Management Agency (FEMA) program concerning building or repairing their home. At the end of the process, if all was done according to the specifications dictated by FEMA, the bank would forgive the loan. Those who had no insurance would incur a 30 percent penalty. How does this help the poor?

FEMA refused to aid us in repairing our destroyed property, claiming that since we lived in another state we did not qualify. The Army Corps of Engineers Levee Breach Claim also asked families of the victims to fill out claim forms and apply for monetary compensation. My family applied, doing everything they asked us to do. We gave birth certificates, death certificates, and everything else requested, but we were denied due to some technicality. They even went as far as to state at the bottom of the denial page that we should not call the court, special master, or court-appointed disbursing agent. After such a complicated task of gathering the required specifications and materials and waiting over a year for a response, we were very disappointed. We put no monetary value on our beloved dad's life; there is none. We only wanted some kind of recompense.

Chapter 5
A Closer Walk with Thee

Deep within my soul, I knew my dad was gone. For hours I poured out my grief before God, yet I could not be comforted. I told myself over and over, *If I were there, I could have saved him.* The thought of him struggling helplessly in the dark waters tortured me. My daddy, the man with whom God blessed us to have for a very long time and whom we felt would go on forever, is gone. The man who protected, defended, and supported us most of our days is gone. He waltzed with my sister at her debutante ball and marched down the church aisle with me on my wedding day—and even with my daughter on her wedding day. He was always there.

I remembered how devastated I had been over the death of
my mother, but the loss of my father was more traumatic. It

was the end of my heritage, the very source of my bloodline. Nevertheless, I believe he is with the Lord and reunited with my mother and sister. During my last visit, Christmas 2004, my stepmother confided in me that Dad knelt at his bedside and prayed morning and night. That was very reassuring to hear. Dad told a newspaper columnist that one of his favorite tunes to play on his tray was "A Closer Walk with Thee" (Dempsey, 1977).

Safe and Secure

Dad was raised to believe in Jesus Christ and often went to the Jesuit cathedral close to his work after performing.

In 1979, after a long, diligent search for truth, I was born again—believing strictly in the Word of God … *sola scriptura*. For years I prayed to statues and said the rosary using beads, believing more in what was tangible than intangible, which opened the door to the occult. I studied psychometry, astrology, and reincarnation; I read tarot cards; I did transcendental meditation, and so on. When life's struggles got worse, these things brought more confusion my way and let me down considerably. On top of all of my problems, my mother's death pushed me over the edge. I embarked on a long, sincere search for truth, but I found a "truth" within itself. Truth did not come easy. It wasn't until incidents happened that were completely out of my control or anyone else's that I really searched for it. Everyone and everything that I believed could remedy my troublesome situations failed me. I had no alternative but to look up. I cried out to Jesus. After all, no one else can answer that call, since Jesus said, "I am the way, the truth and the life, no one comes to the Father except through me" (John 14:6).

I was willing to give up what *I wanted to believe or what I was taught by the world to believe* and accepted whatever Jesus told me, no matter what it was or how I felt about it. Only then was I ready for the truth, and for the first time in my life I understood the Bible. I was spiritually reborn and later baptized into Christ by submergence in water.

On one of my visits to New Orleans, I shared this testimony with my dad, telling him how very *real* Jesus is! I informed Dad that it's not enough to have a mental understanding of who Jesus is or to give verbal affirmation of our faith in Him, but we must *know* Him and have a personal, spiritual link with Him rather than just knowledge of Him. This is the great mystery of the gospel—Christ within! Nicodemus believed in Jesus, but he was not born again of the Holy Spirit. "You must be born again" (John 3:3-6) I asked Dad if he wanted me to pray for him, he said yes. Then I led him in a sinner's prayer, acknowledging his sins to God and asking Jesus to come *into* his heart and be Lord of his life (I John 1:9). Subsequently, my sister was born again a few years before she died and also led Dad in a sinner's prayer; my daughter followed in succession. Lacking biblical knowledge, however, my dad didn't realize that once was enough. Nevertheless, it was better for him to do it three times than not at all. After his spiritual transformation, he took the opportunity to lay hands on the head of the same granddaughter who had led him in a sinner's prayer and bless her.

Dad was like a tired old robot going through the motions of life. He was too healthy to die of natural causes, yet he was caught in a cycle, night after night, faithfully going to Pat O'Brien's. He believed superstitiously that, if he did retire, it would bring on his demise. But what could he do? This psalm of Moses tells us:

> The days of our lives are seventy years; and if by reason of strength they are eighty years, Yet their boast is only *labor* and *sorrow*; for it is soon cut off, And we fly away. (Psalm 90:10)

Lou Gehrig's Disease

Dad had received many blessings in his lifetime, but he also endured much sorrow. He lost his firstborn child, a beautiful baby girl whom he carried in his arms several hours before taking her to the mortuary. The mortician saw him holding a baby and asked to see it. Dad opened the baby's blanket to show him, but the mortician looked puzzled and said, "This baby is dead!" Dad lived to see both his mother and father die as well as two of his sisters. His first daughter died of breast cancer three years prior to the flood, and all of his friends and coworkers passed on. But more grievous than all, he had to watch my mother waste away from a devastating, paralyzing disease. Dad never quite understood the fatality of amyotrophic lateral sclerosis (ALS), also known as Lou Gehrig's disease. It is a deterioration of the nervous system that causes breakdown of the muscle tissues and the spinal cord, thus paralyzing its victims from head to toe. Mother, in her later stages, was unable to speak or move. Dad paid a daytime nurse to help care for her. In everything we did for her, we had to guess what she needed or wanted. I made an alphabet chart to help her to spell out words as I pointed at letters, but that frustrated her. It was heartbreaking! Dad was in denial and tried to be optimistic, looking for her complete recovery. He even tried giving her vitamins and tonics, thinking that might help. Dad had to bathe, feed, and help Mama walk by holding her from behind and pushing each foot, one in front of the other, using his own feet. At times when he could not be there all day, he would sit her in a chair, where she stayed until he returned. Mother kept her condition secret from her children and grandchildren until, one day, she fell and couldn't get up. My daughter, who was home from college at that time, found her and immediately called the neighbors for help. She finally contacted mother's doctor. He said, "Didn't your grandmother tell you?" And he gave her a full report on ALS. My daughter then called us and related Mother's condition to us. We brought my mother to Denver to care for her until the day she passed away. Dad was in a state of shock when we told him Mother had finally succumbed to that longtime, paralyzing condition.

Chapter 6
Television Coverage

Months before the Katrina flood, Dad's favorite dog, You, died of a skin disease. Fortunately, Two in One and Me survived the flood. They were seen on *A Current Affair* on September 8, 2005. Fox News TV propped up a camera on the debris amid the damaged house that was once their loving home. I am thankful for the people from the humane society, who went into the muddy house searching for pets and found homes for the two dogs. A representative of Fox News called me by cell phone while searching Dad's house, yet she told me there was no sign of my dad. There was no red X on his front door to indicate that a body had been found.

Larry King

During the post flood events, my nephew, who was also Dad's first grandson, appeared on a local TV show in New York to talk about the devastation over the drowning of his grandfather. Larry King saw the show and at once contacted him to appear on his show as well. King expressed that he was a fan of my dad's and knew him quite well. *A Current Affair* of Fox also gave a special tribute to Dad. I'm grateful to Larry King and Fox News, which was hosted by Arthel Neville and Tim Green, for the coverage given about my dad, although seeing my dad's picture on TV caused me to break down in tears. Nevertheless, I consider that to be the best eulogy or obituary any family could possibly receive.

Whoopie Goldberg (A Fan)

Many famous fans frequented the popular nightspot. It always excited us children to hear Dad talk of all the movie stars he had met the night before—*Gunsmoke*'s James Arness in particular. Politicians, athletes, and movie stars autographed pictures taken with Dad. They also asked him to autograph their napkins, purses, shirts, and jackets. One fan in particular was the famous comedienne and star of *Ghost* and *Corrina, Corrina*, Whoopie Goldberg. Dad told us that she put a tip of one hundred dollars on his tray and later took a picture with him. I wanted that picture. Unfortunately, it was one of the valuables that perished in the flood. According to my stepmother, nothing from the house was salvageable. Also ruined in the flood, despite hanging on Dad's wall and encased in a large glass frame, was his first tray, encircled by ten thimbles.

Memorial

In January 2006, a memorial service instead of a funeral was held for Dad. His body was never positively identified. I was told to give a DNA sample in Denver, which I did, but it was never used because, the coroner claimed later, the procedure was costly and time consuming. After several months, the coroner from Baton Rouge e-mailed me pictures of items found on the body of an aged man said to have been my dad. Of course, I wanted to see the body, but he said that was impossible because of its condition. The items found on the old man were a gold chain and a copper keychain. They could possibly be things Dad would possess. However, my stepmother reported that he had been dressed for bed when the levy broke, in a white T-shirt and long white boxer shorts. He certainly had no use for a keychain. And the only jewelry he wore was a silver medal of Mary around his neck and his gold wedding band; these were not among the items found. It seemed as if he had done what he said he would do__ "just disappear."

When my sister died in Maryland on March 7, 2002, Dad had insisted that she be flown to New Orleans for burial. Of course, it was more expedient for him to bury her in New Orleans. She had died sixteen days before Dad's ninety-second birthday. It would have been very difficult for him to travel long in an airplane. Traveling with grief in your heart is absolutely draining. I remember how it was for me to fly to New Orleans after hearing that my mother had a fatal disease(ALS); the plane wasn't fast enough! However, my sister and her husband had no plans for burial in New Orleans. While I was at her hospital bedside before she passed, she was adamant about not wanting to be buried in New Orleans. When I asked her why, she said, "Don't ask why!" Could it be that she sensed the future of our beloved city? Even the mausoleums were flooded in Katrina. In 1994, I remembered, she was excited about moving back to New Orleans after being away for twenty-six years. However, when she did move back, she expressed dissatisfaction with the degrading conditions of the city and the demonic forces that she felt while there. Consequently, she was obliged to move back to Maryland.

Nevertheless, Dad was determined to have her buried in New Orleans and willingly gave up his own plot that he had reserved next to my mother, giving no thought for his own place of burial.

Keeping the Legend Alive

Pat O'Brien's will never be the same without Eddie. "He was a legend in his time," remarked his fans. To me, my dad was Mr. New Orleans. One fan of many years expressed my sentiments exactly in a message to my dad inscribed in a book about New Orleans. I omitted the name for the sake of privacy:

> Eddie, because of wonderful people like you, New Orleans is my favorite city in all the world. I thank you so much for being so kind always. You are like a landmark in New Orleans. People come to New Orleans to see Eddie Gabriel at Pat O'Brien's. Therefore, when I saw this book of New Orleans, points of interests, I thought it only fitting that one of New Orleans' best points of interest should have this book.

A tribute to my father was created on a website called Legacy. com by one of his fans for his fans.

Dad's fans from all over the world inquired about his welfare, wanting to know if he had survived the flood. Pat O'Brien's had a special fund-raising celebration in his honor, selling T-shirts with his picture, tapes of his music, and other memorabilia.

My favorite selections of Dad's music can be heard on side two of David Paquette's cassette tape *In and Out of Town*: "The World Is Waiting for the Sunshine" and "Blues My Naughty Sweetie Gives to Me."

Almost a year after the flood, on March 23, 2006, Pat O'Brien's celebrated Eddie Gabriel's birthday by staging a traditional New Orleans's jazz parade called "Keeping the Legend Alive." Such parades start out somber and slow, but then the Dixieland band breaks out into rhythmic jubilation with second liners strutting behind the horse-drawn wagon carrying the casket in the street. I did not attend that celebration because I was still grieving over my dad. My grief was twofold: my father was gone, and the land of my nativity was destroyed. For years I had never failed to visit Pat's to hear my dad play his musical tray. However, at this updated writing, I have traveled back to New Orleans only once since December 2004, in 2007. I can honestly say that I was not ready to face the destruction I saw in my hometown, nor did I visit Pat O'Brien's. Without my dad's smiling face and easy stroll, it would have been too sorrowful for me. Grief is a very perplexing emotion; it comes and goes. You never know when it will hit you, where it will hit you, or what will trigger it.

The year of 2007 was the first time I returned to New Orleans since the Katrina flood. It wasn't until some years later that I was brave enough to even go inside Pat O'Brien's. And even than I felt sadness as I walked to the front entrance. As we walked to the nightclub area, we saw a large picture of my dad at the entrance holding his tray. It made me happy to see him honored. Then we moved on to the patio area and quietly sat for a while. This was during the daytime, which made it a little less painful for me. All of my other visits to see my dad had been at night.

Chapter 7

"Do You Know What It Means to Miss New Orleans?"

The title of this chapter is also that of a song I have sung with fans many times at Pat O'Brien's.

I left New Orleans in the early sixties but loved visiting it every chance I got. I'm grateful to have been born in the city that gave birth to jazz. I learned to love and appreciate all kinds of music. There is no place like it, especially its most palatable food. Chefs take pride in serving the public their best. One doesn't have to search high and low for a good restaurant in New Orleans—they're all good! Being the sixth-largest seaport in the United States, the city manufactured and processed food not found anywhere else in America, especially Creole cream cheese (not cottage cheese). It's the stuff Little Miss Muffet sat down to eat—curds and whey. Dad always had a supply of it for me when he anticipated my visit. The big ships of the Mississippi

River brought to the Big Easy the latest in fashion, music, dances, and trends.

My husband and I loved to visit Café du Monde (Café of the World) in the French Market, which is near the Mississippi River. We would sit and drink *café au lait* and eat beignets, enthralled by the street entertainment around us.

The second-most delightful characteristic of New Orleans is that perpetual feeling of celebration in the air. The people are so connected in every way; everyone seems to be on the same page socially. New Orleans's nicknames are the Big Easy, the Crescent City, and Little Paris, because the French founded it in 1718 and it is primarily French in its tradition and customs. Many streets are named in honor of French explorers. Even the surnames of most New Orleaneans are French. Third, unique to New Orleans is the unmistakable Creole accent. No matter where one might be in the United States, the New Orleans accent can readily be identified in comparison to other Southern accents. It is usually nasal, flat, and as in the French language, the last consonants of words fade out.

Race Relations

Race relations were better in the Crescent City than in many other major Southern cities. The French attitude of "make love, not war" or "live and let live" was still alive in the Big Easy. Under French control and after the Civil War, African Americans gained civil rights and freedom. There were no laws against intermarriage, and people sat where they pleased on public transportation. In 1724, French explorer Bienville promulgated the so-called Code Noir (Black Code), which had been drawn up by the government of Louis XIV, for whom Louisiana was named. This code allowed intermarriage between Europeans and their female slaves or other black female acquaintances (Cowan, Chase, Dufour, LeBlanc, and Wilds, 1983). On November 25, 1895 my maternal grandfather, who was French/Polish, married my grandmother, who was of African descent and from Grenada, Mississippi. They traveled to Mississippi but soon returned to his birthplace, New Orleans, because their union was accepted in the Big Easy. Unfortunately, the Democratic political system initiated segregation and the Jim Crow laws of 1877 (Dufour, 1967), which somewhat destroyed the harmonious race relations in New Orleans.

A Declining City

The New Orleans I grew up in was destroyed long ago. There was a time in New Orleans when the church bells rang at noon and the entire city recessed to pray a prayer called the Angelus.

Catholics in every area of the city stopped what they were doing and knelt to pray. There was also *siesta* time, influenced greatly by the Spanish culture, when an entire community would shut down for rest and naptime. No one dared to work on Sundays.

However, each time I visited my hometown, I witnessed an increase of black poverty. The city, which was once racially and ethnically balanced (Italians, African Americans, French, Germans, Cubans, Filipinos, etc.) became predominantly black. In the past, there were no such areas called ghettos. Blacks lived all over the city, intermingled in neighborhoods—uptown, downtown, and *back-o-town*.

Sensitive Question

I guess because of my evangelical ministry, people confronted me many times with the question, "Do you think Katrina was God's judgment against the city?" I was a little sensitive to that question since my father was one of those who perished in that terrible flood. Evidently, the devastation of Katrina caused even unbelievers to ask questions.

Keeping within biblical interpretation, floods come as a result of judgment; and judgment comes as a result of *violence* and *immorality* (2 Peter 2:4–6), *wickedness* (Genesis 6:5) and *ungodliness* (Psalm 18:4).

Punishment is defined in the *Spirit-Filled Bible* as not so much as a direct action of God's will as "an indirect result of having violated the blessings within the *boundaries* of His will, and thus having exposed ourselves to the judgments outside of it" (p. 848).

Nature has boundaries in respect to the earth. The sea has its place, and so does the land. When either one covers the other, there is disaster. "You have set a boundary that they may not pass over, that they may not return to cover the earth" (Psalm 104:9). The same applies to a society who defies the laws of God.

So, in response to that question, and from a Christian's point of reference, I feel that Katrina was a direct result of man's will acting in direct conflict with God's will. Unfortunately, and as always, the blameless suffer from the moral declension of others. My father lived a long, decent, and prosperous life. And even in death he was blessed to escape suffering long on a sickbed. More floods, tsunamis, earthquakes, and other disasters such as plagues and pestilence are predicted for the entire world. I believe we are in the last days.

The French Quarter

Today, the French Quarter is the focal point of New Orleans. Built on higher ground by the French, it was the first site of the ancient city of New Orleans and suffered very little damage from Katrina. It is currently being used to entice tourists, while the rest of the dilapidated city is still in ruins at this writing. It is also replete with prostitution houses and witchcraft and voodoo shops. As a matter of fact, the city's first public event after the devastating Katrina storm in 2005 was their ninth annual Voodoo Festival in the city park. General admission tickets to this event ranged from $100 to $450.

Followers of Marie Laveaux still visit her grave to this day. They apply big red X's on her tomb as they petition her for favors. I recall one summer in 1989, while gathering information on Marie Laveaux at her gravesite, I observed an affluent-looking middle-aged woman emerge quickly from a black limousine driven by a chauffeur. She was dressed in black, although I could see the serious expression on her face despite its being covered by a black veil. Busily, she walked to Marie Laveaux's tomb, touched it, mumbled a few words, and placed coins in the cracks of the tomb. Without a word, and seriously engrossed in the moment, she walked away, reentered her limousine, and beckoned to her chauffeur to drive on.

My prayer for New Orleans is that no matter how much progress is made to rebuild the city's designated sites and repair the levy, I pray the people will repair the breach that may be between themselves and God.

My Neighborhood Walk

Where houses once stood, there were empty grassy lots. My old neighborhood, which was at one time lively and wholesome, was abandoned and deserted.

Many houses were totally destroyed and barely standing. Any strong tempest could send them tumbling down. I stood in the middle of the block and stared at my old elementary school, which was a large, three-story, red brick building. It was all boarded up. In that block, there had once been a school and seven houses. Now only the school and three homes remained: our childhood home, Dad's childhood home, and my aunt's home. We drove north to see the Ninth Ward house that had belonged to my dad at the time of the Katrina flood. It was also the house in which he had perished. It had been renovated. However, the devastation in the Ninth Ward was heartbreaking! What did I see? In a word … emptiness!

I started writing this book in 2006. Oftentimes I'd put it off because it put me in a sad frame of mind. However, my determination to give tribute and pay homage to my dad is paramount. This day, August 29, 2007, marks the second anniversary of his death and the destructive Katrina flood. My granddaughter called me from Louisiana to encourage me. I was inspired by that phone call to start writing again, pushing myself to accomplish what I intended two years ago.

Photo Gallery

My dad, me and my husband Adrian in front of Pat O' Brien's

after celebrating my Dillard University 40th alumni reunion

My sister Garcia, Dad, and son-in-law David at Pat O' Brien's

Me, Dad, my daughter Lisa at Dad's 80th Birthday celebration at Pat O' Brien's

Mom and Dad at the horse races

Mom and Dad at my sister Garcia's Debutante Ball

Me with my Dad sitting at the table in Pat O'Brien's nightclub

having a Hurricane drink on Mardi Gras Day.

Works Cited

Angus Lind, "91 and Still Clickin," *Times-Picayune*, March 23, 2001, pp. E-1 and E-10.

Angus Lind, "Iron Man Still Going Strong," *Times-Picayune*, December 5, 1987, n.p.

Jack Dempsey, "Tapping Turns on Tips for Rhythm King," *New Orleans Item-Tribune*, May 16, 1977, B-1.

Charles L. Dufour, *New Orleans: The Crescent City*. New York: Arts, Inc., 1967, pp. 30 and 35.

Joseph Arceneaux Jr., *Biography of Professor Medard H. Nelson, 1850–1933*, New Orleans, LA 1987.

Lewis Grizzard, "The Place, and a Musical Drink Tray," *Atlanta Constitution*, January 11, 1978, p. 1-C.

Raymond J. Martinez and Jack Holmes. *New Orleans: Facts and Legends*, New Orleans: Hope Publications, 2014, p. 61.

Walter G. Cowan, John C. Chase, Charles Dufour, O.K. LeBlanc, and John Wilds, *New Orleans Yesterday and Today: A Guide to the Deity,* Baton Rouge & London: Louisiana State University Press, 1983, pp. 183, 185.

About the Author

As a first time author, she wanted to use her talent for the purpose giving glory and honor to her departed famous Father. She is a Christian woman, a wife, mother, grandmother and retired teacher.